AVOIDING

HEDGEHOG SCENARIO

Telling stories of practical evangelism

Philip A. Clarke

CLIFF COLLEGE PUBLISHING

British Library Cataloguing in Publication Data.
A catalogue record for this book is available
from the British Library.

ISBN 1 898362 23 8

Printed by:

MOORLEY'S Print & Publishing
23 Park Rd., Ilkeston, Derbys DE7 5DA
Tel/Fax: (0115) 932 0643

from data supplied on disk

CONTENTS

Children's Holiday Club, Skerries, Near Dublin

Open-Air Praise, Rochdale Town Centre

4

INTRODUCTION

In teaching courses on evangelism at Cliff College and a variety of other theological institutions, I am well aware that this subject is only meaningful and authentic when put into practice. Indeed, my students often remind me of the fact! Sadly, for many Christians evangelism, the sharing of faith with the intention that people make their own response to the Gospel of Jesus Christ, is rather an embarrassment. Some enthusiasts, intending to urge and inspire, send their hearers on guilt trips. My intention here is to offer accessible models for witness, which give confidence in the message and the task.

Evangelism is not 'for experts only' but is the task of every Christian. Helpful insights can be gained from the many books on the subject, but there is no substitute for simply taking a risk and 'having a go'. Sharing faith must never be monochrome in style, artificial, patronising or blinkered in its world view. Some people have a special gift in explaining and expressing the Gospel, but all Christians are witnesses. As the early Christians exclaimed: 'We cannot but tell....' It is impossible to keep Good News under wraps.

But beware all you activists! It is God's church and God's mission, not ours. We are called to be partners with Him in His work. All the faith sharing stories which follow are against the back cloth of what God has done in Christ and what He is doing in our world today. We do not take God into these situations. Rather, we find Him there already, sometimes in the darkest or most unlikely places. With this mind set, there is potential for both the teller and the hearer to be transformed by the Gospel.

This book first appeared as a series of articles in the Methodist Recorder in 1998-99, with the double-edged title of 'Practically Evangelism.' This incorporated the notion of almost (but not quite). Stories of ordinary people, whose lives God uses in the multi-faceted work of sharing faith, draw out key issues for mission. Questions for group discussion conclude each chapter. As you read, perhaps you will say ' I could do that...' I have endeavoured to keep this emphasis in the new title. Story telling is in vogue. The twelve stories selected offer specific insights on mission in a new millennium. In this way 'telling stories' are told.

When leading mission consultations for congregations large and small throughout Britain, I avoid succumbing to any desire for quick fix solutions to complex long-term challenges. However, I am invariably and understandably asked for ideas and stories of 'things that work' elsewhere. Given that I have only a snapshot of any of these contexts, I am happy to offer varied styles and models of mission to stimulate specific creative action. Whilst God works in His way in His mission, He also works through people and there is no limit to the impact that one person can have, even to change a nation.

Think for instance of Rosa Parkes, a black woman in Alabama who, in the 1960's, sat in the 'whites only' section of a bus. Refusing to move, her action sparked a bus boycott which in time changed the laws of a state and the attitudes of a nation. You have often heard of Martin Luther King but the principles of God's rule are brought about as much through 'ordinary' people as through those in the public eye. Our life and our story can make a difference.

Confidence is what we need - confidence in the Gospel and in the God who embodies it in His Son and commissions us to declare it by His Spirit. Then we will do more than the poor hedgehog scurrying through the darkness, transfixed by perceived oncoming disaster into fatal inertia.

Cliff College Students from around the world
India – UK – South Africa

1. SWITCH ON - TUNE IN

'Are you professionally boring or just a gifted amateur?' enquires local broadcaster Gini Carlin, beginning a West Yorkshire Classic Gold religious news and views programme which she has been helping to present from a Bradford studio. She has recently received two awards for her work at the CACLB, (Churches Advisory Council for Local Broadcasting) annual conference at Swanwick. Gini intends to continue her radio work as an extension of her ministry as a member of the evangelistic team at Cliff College, Derbyshire.

Many Christians come across as just plain boring. Not so Gini Carlin as she slices through the religious jargon and stuffy church diaries saying to her listeners: 'I'm the one who wrote in for a book on the Toronto blessing because I thought it was about the Lone Ranger and his best mate!'.

Local Radio listeners want entertainment, she says, 'which is a lot more radical than Cosy Corduroy Music - I'm from a different world to you ... Most religious broadcasting makes me feel like an outsider.... If I hear the word diocese again I'll.... It sounds like a solution for loose bowels...'

To be noticed the Gospel needs to be set free from 'religious slots' in our lives and in the media and to be lively, relevant, contemporary and jargon free.

The style may not be quite Radio 4 but it certainly grabs attention - 'Make an effort to understand my world' she says on behalf of the unchurched listener. The world of soap operas, demanding children, tough jobs and noisy neighbours. Many religious programmes say more about garden fetes and church bells than real issues. Most people are not disinterested in the Gospel, often they are looking for hope or some kind of spirituality, but they are turned off by the way the message is packaged. The church seems, and is, largely irrelevant to their situation.

Religious broadcasting, especially on existing secular channels rather than only through 'Christian Channels ', offers tremendous opportunities for ordinary people with a passion for Jesus and a story to tell. Gini is 25 and from the village of Wingerworth near Chesterfield. After two years as a student at Cliff College she worked for a year in Colchester as a lay worker in the Methodist Circuit with particular involvement in youth outreach before returning to Cliff as a member of the evangelistic team. She has always been a fan of local radio and first had experience of presenting material on the air through hospital radio getting the Gospel message across in bite sized chunks. It's not half as terrifying as you might imagine - 'Speak as though you are talking to one other person' (i.e. converse rather than preach) is the usual advice. You may have an interesting snippet of news or an opinion on a contemporary issue. Be bold, be positive and contact one of your local radio stations - you never know what opportunities it may open up. How much more effective is evangelism that happens in the public arena rather than in the safety of church buildings, and that it connects with our sound bite culture declaring the unchanging Gospel in a language that people understand and relate to.

The image of the church which comes across through the media is often negative. Church people and especially church leaders are depicted as either whimps or freaks in popular entertainment but too frequently the real thing doesn't look too different from the characterisation! How much we need the creative, humorous, punchy style of Gini and others like her on local radio to reach the parts that Sunday sermons never reach.

Gini ends one broadcast with a description of her visit to the dentist - dreaded moment! That is until she met him - young and handsome, not at all what she had expected. Some people's picture of God is a little like that: off putting, fearful, to be avoided - but the real encounter dispels the false image. What could be better than to spend twenty minutes looking into his eyes with your mouth wide open! A new slant on the God we worship, local radio style.

THINK THROUGH
1. *How can we speak the world's language in order to connect with a non-church culture?*
2. *How can the media be used to enable Christian witness?*

BIBLE BASE
Psalm 137 v.4 - Knowing how to sing the Lord's song is a challenge for the Jews in Babylon and for us today.

Drama in Worship – Rochdale

2. COME OVER TO BRITAIN AND HELP US

There are not too many links between Kabale and Leeds but Stephen Tirwomwe is one of them.

Stephen arrived in Britain two years ago sponsored by the Church Missionary Society (CMS) to work as a mission partner in the parish of Osmondthorpe not far from the centre of Leeds. He is married to Margaret and they have brought with them to cool damp Northern England and to this somewhat troubled council housing estate, their children Solomon, Simon, Gladys and Geraldine, leaving behind in Uganda their two eldest children Samson and Gloria who are completing their high school education.

The family arrived in Leeds a year ago and Stephen began research at Leeds University one day per week. This research involves a comparative study of missionary congregations in Britain and Uganda. Five days a week he works in the Osmondthorpe area with the local parish church sharing faith and getting alongside people in the community. On Sundays he shares the leading of worship and preaches at the Anglican church on the estate where from a very small base the congregation is growing. Margaret leads a Sunday School class. When they arrived at the church their family instantly doubled the size of the Sunday School but now their own children are bringing friends along and putting Stephen and Margaret in touch with parents.

Between 1985 and 1988 Stephen studied at Bishop Tucker Theological College, Mukono, Uganda for a BD before becoming co-ordinator for the Diocese of Kigezi. In 1993-94 Stephen studied at All Nations Christian College, Ware, Hertfordshire for an MA before returning to Uganda to be Acting Principal at Bishop Tucker Theological College. Stephen is amazed by the social differences he observes between Osmondthorpe and Hertfordshire. 'It is like two different countries,' he says. He is grappling with the problems of genuine poverty on a daily basis in Osmondthorpe but finds the people warm and welcoming.

In answering the question, 'Why is your church growing in this difficult area?', Stephen's response is that 'people come to church through friendship.' Some are looking for hope - there's not much scope for complacency on this estate - people are battling to survive. 'As soon as we arrived we opened the door of our home - though we have to be very careful. We are happy to have visits from people around and through that friendship some of them have come to church and others have just come to see this man who has come from Africa! Soon after we arrived an old man came to me and asked me to conduct his wife's funeral. When he came to the church, he was attracted and has become a friend and come to the Bible study in our house. He is 87 years old. He feels supported by the Lord and by our family.'

'Another reason for growth is that we are committed to prayer. We meet every morning to pray and share the word of God and we have a monthly meeting for prayer for two hours in the evening. My hope is to enable the congregation to understand that it is their task to do mission - mission is to do with the whole of church life. I always ask the Parochial Church Council (PCC) 'Why does this church exist if it cannot identify itself with the community?'. How do they reflect the Christian life in clubs and on the streets? I'm challenging the British reservedness about not interfering in other people's business. Jesus interfered in the world by becoming a man - we must be influenced by this doctrine of incarnation - we must share through our speaking. Jesus will judge British culture if it inhibits the sharing of the Gospel.'

Stephen sees friendship evangelism as crucial. 'How many friends do you have with whom you could share the Gospel?' he asks. 'We can expect that people will think that the Christian witness is offensive or patronising but we must still share the Good News.' His hope for St Philip's Church, Osmondthorpe, is that after five years when he returns to Uganda he will leave behind a missionary congregation. 'Ultimately the Church Council are the leaders of the church - they know the area and understand the culture so they should be the most effective missionaries here'.

'We have started a youth group and they are going to be mainly involved in music but there is also an input of Christian teaching. They meet every Wednesday.' The Sunday congregation has doubled in twelve months after a period of long term decline. Stephen is now able to put this experience alongside his observation of other congregations around Britain and Ireland in his part-time role as project worker for the national research initiative 'Building Bridges of Hope.' Through this he sees that there is no blue print for effective evangelism, rather that different things work in different locations. Prayer and faith sharing however always come out high as features of effective missionary congregations. Above all, it is clear that one family living for Christ can have a powerful effect on their environment - and that is how churches grow.

THINK THROUGH
1. *What are the main cultural barriers to the Gospel in Britain?*
2. *What can Christians in our culture learn from Christians in another culture to empower their witness?*
3. *Why does your church exist?*
4. *Identify situations in which you would be an 'outsider' - How do you feel in these situations?*
5. *Friendship builds bridges where people feel they do not 'belong'. Brainstorm the characteristics of friendship.*

BIBLE BASE
Acts 16 v.9 - 'Come over to Macedonia and help us'. Where might 'Macedonia' be for us? Is it where you are now or where God calls you to go?

10

3. BY ALL MEANS

The saying goes that 'farmers never retire.' In the case of Bill and Mary Parkinson of Old Vicarage Farm, Bartle near Preston in Lancashire that is true, but in a different sense.

Bill decided to retire from dairy farming fifteen years ago, but far from sitting back and taking life easy this enabled him to take on more preaching responsibilities throughout the North West of England and, with his wife Mary, to become host and hostess for Methodist holidays in many parts of Britain.

He looks back at his days in farming as very demanding - though he has no regrets about following in his family's tradition of dairying. He speaks with feeling about the way BSE has 'knocked the sparkle out of farming' and of the great need for farmers to have people to talk to who understand their difficulties. Whilst farming has always had great significance in their lives, they have not allowed it to dominate. After milking fifty cows or attending to the needs of a growing family it was common for Bill and Mary to be off to run the children's club at their local village church or for Bill to be travelling long distances to preach. Because farming and preaching are such different roles, Bill says involvement in one helped him avoid burnout in the other. He always fears growing stale. 'I'm continually asking God to keep me fresh,' he says and 'taking disappointments to God in prayer.'

Bill has always considered himself an ordinary man who takes some risks for God. One of his favourite scriptures is Acts 9 concerning Ananias courageously visiting Saul of Tarsus and explaining the Christian way to him after the Damascus Road experience. Bill and Mary are living testimony to a God who takes ordinary lives offered to him and does something wonderful with them and through them.

Bill's preaching style, honed over fifty years as a Methodist Local Preacher, is very much that of the traditional evangelist, learned from his brief time as a student and then evangelist at Cliff College. He left the College in 1951, having learned many things about the Bible, but of special importance was discovering how to help people come to faith. Not that this was some mystical technique. It was much more to do with a genuine love for people as we find them and a passion to see them come to know Jesus in a personal way. The ministry of Ernest Steele and Jim Beasley, Cliff Evangelists at that time, impressed him enormously and gave him a basis for his future work.

Styles of preaching and evangelism have changed. Bill observes, there has been a switch in preaching from formal challenge to more conversational styles. ' There is no substitute for preaching,' he says, ' but we must use modern methods.' House groups have been another important focus of Bill and Mary's work for more than thirty years. Their farmhouse has hosted Bible study groups and youth gatherings where many have come to faith. A busy working life never deterred them from offering hospitality, a warm welcome and a listening ear. Business contacts, family and friends all knew of Bill and Mary's faith. This kind of relational witness they feel is the way forward in evangelism. Open hearts and open homes are not beyond any of us. Their greatest thrill has been to see people coming to know Jesus as Lord and Saviour through their witness.

Since retiring from farming, this ministry of hospitality and pastoral care has developed in new ways. When they were invited to be hosts for Methodist Guild Holidays and Methodist Holiday Hotels, it seemed at first an unlikely move, but Bill and Mary have felt thoroughly fulfilled in sharing this ministry together over the past fifteen years in a way that full time farming could never have allowed. Some years they have hosted seven times, more recently only three times. As holidaymakers relax and unwind in the comfort of their hotel they are often ready to share spiritual needs and experience. Bill and Mary have been there to listen, counsel and pray on many occasions and have helped and encouraged many. A far cry perhaps from Bill's days as a Cliff College Trekker in the streets and on the beaches in the immediate post war years, yet effective evangelism and ministry in context all the same. Working life, evangelism and pastoral care are an effective trinity.

THINK THROUGH
1. *How does your faith impact on your work?*
2. *If God has given you some 'bonus years', what are your goals in extra time?*
3. *Gifts of hospitality and preaching are not always valued in the same way. Which gifts do you have? - Ask someone else to identify these for you. How can they be used?*

BIBLE BASE
Genesis 15 - God used Abraham (mainly) in his old age.

Gospel Cookery in a Preston Pub

4. SEIZE THE DAY

'Don't stand around in the church kitchen - you never know what might happen.' That is the advice of John Smith, a member of Thrum Hall Methodist Church in Rochdale, for it was there that God called him to Romania.

John, head teacher of a Primary School, was off work recovering from a stress-related illness and was just getting back to his old self. Having become a Christian about a year before, John was seeking some sense of direction in his life away from a successful teaching career. Standing there in the church kitchen, he was challenged by a friend to assist with driving a vanload of donated goods to Romania. He agreed to be involved. The trip was to change his life.

It became the first of twelve trips to Romania under the auspices of the charity Spurgeon's Child Care, a charity supported by his local congregation. John's professional experience of children, parents and administrative matters offered invaluable skills in this new opportunity and he has subsequently become International Co-ordinator for the charity. He has led teams and helped initiate new family centre work in some of the poorest parts of Romania, Moldova, Uganda and Mexico. The enormous growth of the work of Spurgeon's Childcare is an indication of the need for work with children and families around the world but is also a tribute to the quality of the service offered. Whilst giving has increased, the expansion of the work is limited by financial constraints. John says that, because Spurgeon's Child Care will not use lottery funds, finances are stretched.

There is a merging of evangelism and social action in these family centre projects. Whilst the family centres are open to everyone in Romania, a predominantly Orthodox country, there is Christian teaching and many people have come to a personal faith in Christ through seeing faith in action. Highlights of the work for John have been numerous but among them he speaks of helping to build a children's playground and seeing three hundred children having the time of their lives on it the moment it was completed. He is always impressed by the way the Gospel crosses cultural frontiers. He finds that personal faith in Christ brings unity amidst cultural diversity. So much so that, after so many visits to Romania, each visit feels like coming home. John's wife Mags and sons Michael and Andrew are supportive of his work despite the periods away from home that it entails.

One of the exciting spin-offs of his involvement with Spurgeon's Child Care has been the opportunity to involve fellow members in his home church in Rochdale in various projects. Several members from Thrum Hall Methodist Church have visited projects, helped run holiday clubs, built play equipment, assisted with driving vehicles etc. It really has been a great team building opportunity and tremendously enriching of faith and cross-cultural understanding.

The congregation themselves are sponsoring a family centre and those who are unable to travel to Romania in person support the work financially and in prayer. Working together for specific goals, whether equipment for a kindergarten or grass seed for a football field, captures people's imagination and puts overseas mission in a new dimension.

John is well aware of the need to avoid aid dependence in the recipients. He says that slowly there is evidence that attitudes of receivers and givers are changing towards team responsibility. He cites examples of a local bakery donating bread and a paint manufacturer giving quantities of paint to help the family centre in its community. However, outside the Christian community, John finds that years of oppression and corruption have bred distrust of other people. Christians have the opportunity to model a different way. Spurgeon's Child Care aim to keep families together wherever possible and to provide basic education and a snack meal at the centres. They also offer social work and medical advice and distribute food and clothing. Ten centres have been opened by Spurgeon's since 1992. These can be run for as little as £400 per month including staff salaries - inflation is a huge problem in Romania.

There is generally a great openness to the Gospel in Romania, John finds, in contrast with comfortable and complacent British society. He is uncertain how the work will develop in the future though he hopes for a consolidation of existing projects rather than a proliferation of work which cannot be adequately sustained. Looking back on the past five years he is amazed at the way in which the Lord has led him - and it all started over the washing up in the church kitchen!

THINK THROUGH
1. *Try communicating with someone else in the room without using words and then discuss a time when God seemed to be telling you important things. What was your response?*
2. *How do we distinguish God's call from our own wishes?*
3. *How can we put social action and evangelism together?*
4. *What opportunities and risks may God be calling us to?*
5. *Think of occasions when one person's vision has inspired others.*

BIBLE BASE
The Book of Ruth shows how cultural barriers are overcome.

One to One Witness – Teignmouth, Devon

5. MEETING GOD IN THE SHOWER
(AND OTHER PLACES)

If you have the impression that the Christian message is a little tame meet Kim Tek Goh. Kim was born in Singapore and as a young man travelled to America in search of adventure and to leave some problems behind. He soon 'got in with the wrong set' and turned increasingly to crime. He travelled around the United States including the beautiful island of Hawaii. Unsettled and dissatisfied, one night he threw a dart at a map of the world. It landed on Lisbon - Kim packed his belongings and followed the dart.

Travelling around Europe he came to Britain. He became involved in the protection rackets operated by the Triads, the Chinese Mafia. Crime landed him in gaol in West Yorkshire. He had never had much time for religion but, after an argument with the minister taking the service at the prison, he had a modern day 'Damascus Road experience' suddenly and powerfully encountering the power of God in the shower room. This experience was a turning point for Kim and his life began to change out of all recognition. Having left prison and determined to go on with God he became a student at Cliff College and later married the Principal's secretary! Now he is a Methodist Local Preacher, has completed a B.A. degree in Biblical and Evangelistic Ministry and is training to be a Methodist Minister! Who said that Christians are boring?

Your testimony may not be entirely similar to Kim's! - It is no less valid to have a gradual journey of faith. What you do with your story is the important thing. In an age which is hooked on individual experience, intrigued by spiritual journeys and fascinated by stories with human interest, Christians have an amazing opportunity to tell their story of faith - not all at one time or according to some pre-packed formula relating mostly to what happened years ago but in contemporary bite sized chunks and awake to God's timing; knowing what to say, how to say it and when to say it. Effective witnessing to the Gospel of God's grace often starts with sharing our own story.

Kim tells his story in an unusual way. For several years he worked as a chef in a Chinese restaurant. Now he uses these skills to give cookery demonstrations in pubs, colleges, churches, youth clubs and homes. Sometimes this has been linked to Alpha courses, on other occasions the cookery has been part of a night school course or a community activity. As he chops the ingredients with astonishing speed he tells how once he used such knives to chop people. As the wok heats up and the ingredients are mixed and cooked he shows how God can forgive people who have made mistakes and give them a new beginning. Then it's time to taste - Yes, 'taste and see that the Lord is good.'

What skills has God given you to use? Are there some opportunities for you to tell your story, not so much the story of how you came to faith some years ago, but how God is real to you today. Many people will argue with your ideas, ask difficult questions about suffering, other religions, hypocrisy in high places (things about which we must be prepared to speak) - but they cannot deny your personal experience of God.

Research by Bishop John Finney during this Decade of Evangelism has shown that 85% of people who come to Christian faith do so through the witness of a friend. How much more value therefore must we put on our own story? The more ordinary that seems to us, the more it is likely to connect with our friends and neighbours. Don't be misled into thinking that dramatic testimony is the only or even the most effective tool. Our nation will hear the Good News in a language they understand only when ordinary people share their story of encountering the great story of the Gospel. This story spills out of our lives in words and actions as we go about our daily lives. In Matthew 10 v. 9 Christ says, 'As you are going' share the Gospel. That does not mean, when the church is ready, when my life is perfect, when I have more time, when I've seen the video or read the latest book on the subject, or understood more theology - just that as we live our lives the Gospel seeps through.

Too often we wait for the mega opportunity, the crisis moment, the special event, the inspiring speaker. Actually, we are the witnesses. The treasure is in jars of clay (2 Corinthians 4) but it IS there - outwardly unimpressive - inwardly refreshing and life changing

Whether you met God in the prison showers or the Sunday School hall, your story counts. Don't keep it to yourself. Share first with someone who will be a sympathetic listener, listen to his or her story and then enter into dialogue. Don't give the impression that you have somehow 'arrived'. Speak more in terms of journey and avoid religious language - be yourself and see what God can do.

THINK THROUGH
1. *Tell your story - especially if it seems 'ordinary'.*
2. *Does sudden crisis or gradual process best describe your journey of faith?*

BIBLE BASE
Acts 9 - A classic conversion story and its sequel.

6. A HYMN, A PRAYER AND A TELLING OFF
(AND OTHER APPROACHES TO CHILDREN'S EVANGELISM)

Children's work has sometimes been a Cinderella aspect of evangelism. Some feel that children are too young and impressionable to make their own response to the Gospel and fear manipulative methods. Many churches, aware of their lack of young people, seek to appoint a youth worker, yet they are often trying to contact a group who have already become alienated from the church. We must focus energy in the earlier years.

Children's missioner Claire Morgans recalls a large church which held an outreach event in a marquee hoping to attract the local community. The local community arrived in the guise of a group of ten year old boys who attempted to cut the guy ropes of the marquee with pen knives. Eventually these 'trouble makers' were invited into the marquee where they heard and responded to the challenge to follow Jesus. The next day they returned with a disabled friend, his legs in callipers. 'Will you pray for him?' they asked. 'Jesus will make him better, won't he?' Diffidently, the leaders agreed to pray. The boy took off the callipers and began to walk unaided. He returned with his parents the next day seeking explanations.

Whilst the Methodist Church has a good record in children's work, this has often been mainly in terms of Sunday School, uniformed groups and mid-week clubs. These are important but it is clear that often they give children a taste of the Christian story whilst assuming that their role is merely preliminary to the main work of discipleship and adult church membership. Sunday morning is now probably the worst time to try to run a children's meeting - so many are visiting Dad, away for the weekend, playing football, riding horses - or just in bed! We need to offer more mid-week options for children to hear the Good News in a language they relate to, then take their responses seriously.

Claire recalls a conversation with a seven year old who was eager to follow Jesus. 'Go away and think about it,' was the advice given by the leader. The next morning the little girl was back saying, 'I've thought about it and I want to be a friend of Jesus'. Children's workers and others will often remind the congregation that the children are the church of today not just of tomorrow but we still work in a way that suggests that we believe the opposite in terms of changes in worship, use of buildings, finance and resources. Children may not be capable of grasping the intricacies of the Apostles Creed (who is?) but, if we believe that faith is more about relationship than information, we must find ways to be fully inclusive of all ages. Our children's work must be more than colouring pictures and telling stories from the Bible. There must be an intention to help children experience Jesus for themselves.

Alongside the well known weekly teaching materials, SALT from Scripture Union, David C. Cook, Partners in Learning etc, there is a good range of holiday club packs (again from S.U.). Of these, Story Keepers, has some excellent video material introducing Bible themes and characters in the context of the persecution of Christians by the Romans in the late first century. The theme running through is the way in which they passed on the stories about Jesus, and by implication, how we can do the same. It conveys, in cartoon form, the excitement of the Christian life and the life changing impact of Jesus' encounter with the people of his day. We live in a multi-media world - except for work with the youngest children, keep the flannelgraph set in the cupboard!

Claire and Mark Morgans have been involved in children's ministry in a variety of contexts in Llandudno, Lancashire, Bristol, Cliff College and at Easter People. They are currently in Rugby where Mark is minister of three churches; children's evangelism plays an important part in their work. Claire has recently written two resource books for children's' workers based on her own experiences. The games ideas are 'wild' and the overriding aim is to introduce children to Jesus as their best friend.

Small group work with children is an important aspect of Claire's work. She advocates running a fortnightly or monthly children's' house group of an interactive style with lots of activities: baking, trips and games alongside praise, prayer and Christian teaching. Music is an important part of this approach and modern songs are the most effective. We have moved on from 'Bind us Together', 'Shine Jesus Shine' and 'Majesty'! She encourages team work and sometimes involves people who would not see themselves as 'good with children'. As part of a holiday club team, they can use their skills, perhaps painting scenery, handling publicity or preparing food and drinks. In this way they gain an enthusiasm for the work with children, discover that they enjoy it and become more involved, gaining much from the experience. She points to instances where those who became involved at the level of pouring orange squash ended up running the week of holiday club activities a few years down the line.

The responses of children at such events are amazing - simple, profound and amusing all at the same time ...   'If God is so big he is everywhere and he lives inside us, why doesn't he show through', 'Am I blessed?' ... 'Is my rabbit in heaven?' ... 'I had earache so I prayed and it went away' ... 'Here is some money (71p) for the poor people'....

Claire finds that music and drama presentations, whilst very demanding of leaders, are effective in reaching parents. Schools are often suprisingly open to offers to share in the leading of assembly.

Again, this is best done on a team basis where less confident members can gain experience and courage from others in the team. If a regular assembly slot is possible, then the team model is more and more important and helps children and teachers to see that the church is willing to meet them on their own ground, not just in a church building. This works well in ethnically and religiously mixed schools where the headteacher is supportive and the type of presentation offered is appropriate. We need to avoid assemblies that replicate our own bad experiences of school 'worship' - a hymn, a prayer and a telling off is not the most positive introduction to faith. There is a huge amount of good contemporary school assembly material getting across lively and varied themes from a Christian point of view - so there is no excuse for the presentation to look tired, boring or unrelated to real life.

It is the lament of many children's workers that they visit too many churches where the stewards complain to the youngsters about skateboarding in the church car park and then wonder why there are so few of them in the pews on Sunday. There are however some inspirational examples of congregations which have snipped the barbed wire between church and the young generation: opening drop-in facilities, running play schemes and holidays, offering after school care, supporting single parents, training football teams, establishing cyber cafes, encouraging bands... Thank God for this diversity and that many come to faith through the dedicated and prayerful commitment of ordinary people with a love for children.

THINK THROUGH
1. *Did you begin to follow Christ as a child? Share your story.*
2. *Are there some new styles of children's work which would be appropriate in your situation?*
   Is your church's work with children on Sunday more about colouring than discipling?
3. *What can the faith of a child teach us?*
4. *How do you feel about the children in your neighbourhood?*

BIBLE BASE
1 Samuel 3 - The Lord calls Samuel as a child.

Children's Camp,
Haapsalu, Estonia

Drop-in Coffee Morning,
Uttoxeter

All Age Worship,
Rochdale

7. VET ON THE FRONT LINE - IN MISSION

Featured in innumerable TV series, the life and work of the country vet, at least in its sanitised and glamorised form, has been widely known since James Herriott's classic books. Chris Swift, a vet in a Penrith (Cumbria) practice for 17 years does not fit the standard model.

Chris was brought up in North Lancashire and trained in veterinary medicine at Cambridge before coming north to Penrith to join a practice dealing mainly with farm animals but also with family pets. He became a Christian whilst at university and at an early stage faced the dilemma of whether he should, as a Christian, be more concerned to offer medical help to humans than animals. He concluded that he was called to this particular role, completed his training and eventually came to the growing veterinary practice where he is now a partner.

From time to time, Chris has considered whether he should leave his present employ to take up 'full time Christian work' - unfortunate terminology and often wrongly applied. He continues however to find fulfilment in his work and significant opportunities to share his faith with colleagues and clients - evangelising cows is not something which he has yet perfected! Whilst Chris does not deny that the thought of spending more time in overtly Christian work is attractive, he feels that he is called to 'blossom where he is planted.' He may be the only Christian those he meets in his working life ever get to know on a long term basis. Indeed, it is this 'long term' witness to which Chris is deeply committed. He hopes to see people receive Christ as Lord of their lives, but he knows that first he must work at being a friend, earning the right to speak about the Gospel rather than crashing in with a mouth full of religious clichés. Putting the Gospel into action and being there for people are central to Chris's approach to faith sharing. Being a friend to people first and foremost because we care about them not just because he wants them to come to church!

Chris, and thousands like him, are the real 'full time Christian workers' - involved with ordinary people in the work place and the community, they live out what they believe and speak it out where there is opportunity, rather than standing outside the main stream of life and shouting the Gospel from a distance in a language that has no relevance to and therefore no impact. There has been a tendency in the church to give the task of evangelism mainly to inexperienced 'outsiders' - individuals or teams that are here for a ten day mission or a twelve month project and then away again. These things may be helpful within the overall plan of a church's mission but the main work of witness must be on-going, indigenous and incarnational - to the community from within the community: costly, measured, intentional, consistent - in there for the long haul.

In the nine vet practice, Chris feels that his main witness is to his colleagues more than to his clients - largely because of the long term continuity that this involves. It has dawned on him over many years that his work IS his ministry. His Christian service is not what he does in his spare time or directly connected with church - it is the whole of his life, being and doing, in business and relaxation, work and family. 'Why', he asks, 'do we never get sermons about work?' Presumably, because some preachers have little contemporary experience of the work context and others have a view of discipleship which ignores or fails to connect with working life.

He seeks help, support and understanding of his work situation so that he can more effectively address the challenges and opportunities it offers. How can he help his hard pressed farmer clients with their insurance claims for cattle without being dishonest? Where is the forum to discuss these issues? How can he balance irregular working hours including so many disrupted nights and weekends with family life? His wife June and their three young sons Matthew, Samuel and Ned deserve more time than his work commitments allow and he knows that his first responsibility is to care for them.

Chris and June help to lead a youth fellowship, a home group and an Alpha course. The boys are involved in children's activities at Penrith Methodist Church. It's an action packed life - and it's ALL about mission.

THINK THROUGH
1. *Sometimes we attempt to shut God out of some parts of our lives. Do you see God as active in your working life?*
2. *How can you best be a witness for Christ in your work place or some other 'secular' context?*
3. *How can church better relate to the whole of life?*
4. *Make a prayer list of the work places and work colleagues of the people in your group.*

BIBLE BASE
Colossians 2 v.6-8 - Consistent Christian living is the best witness.

8. UNLIKELY MESSENGERS

Ever felt you've been buried alive? Perhaps you sometimes feel that you are the most unlikely person for God to use? Maybe you feel you are 'past your prime' and have taken too many knocks on life's journey or you are simply living in some obscure back water? Let God surprise you as he has Eva McCullouch!

Eva's mother died when she was very young. Her drunken father abused her, made her eat her meals in the garage and made her feel she was rubbish. Her escape was to get married but some of the same problems recurred. She and her three young children found themselves homeless. Friends from the local chapel in Cramlington, Northumberland helped her rebuild her life, offering friendship and furniture, nurturing her in a faith re-born in desperate times. The children grew up, moved away from home and gave Eva time to ask where her life was headed. She was encouraged to spend a year at Cliff College where her ability to share her faith out of the tough experiences of her own life grew. Arriving at the college in fear and trepidation, all too aware of her complete lack of academic qualifications, she blossomed passing the Certificate course in Biblical and Evangelistic ministry. At the end of the year at Cliff (1995-96) she felt a clear call to continue in evangelistic work. She spent a year with Derbyshire Village Mission based in the small community of Winster near Matlock, working in a team engaged in supporting and encouraging local churches in their outreach to all sections of village life.

After twelve months, the team disbanded as the work of Derbyshire Village Mission moved to other areas within the county. Eva however, still supported in prayer and finance by her sending congregation in Northumberland, continued to live in Winster, obtained a part time job as a carer and took up residence in a small flat on the main street. With no car and minimal finance, she intends to stay in the village until God tells her otherwise. Her home is a place with an open door of friendship in the name of Jesus. She shares fellowship with members of the three congregations in the village, Methodist, Wesleyan Reformed and Anglican, in a variety of ways. Her week is packed with small group leadership in homes, pastoral visiting, running children's clubs and training as a Local Preacher. She combines a deep understanding of people and empathy with their struggles with a heart for evangelism, missing no opportunity to share her faith in natural, largely conversational ways.

Prominence and pedigree have never been commensurate with effectiveness for the Kingdom of God. The real saints are the 'unknown' and 'unlikely' company of Christian people whose faithfulness and sincerity challenges us all. Such commitment is not beyond any of us. It is motivated not by guilty conscience or a kind of relentless evangelical activism but by love - love of God and love of people.

This cannot be manufactured, it comes by years of scholarship in the school of hard knocks and dedicated prayerful discipleship, reading the Word, living it out, telling it forth.

There are times when Eva, like most of us, feels inundated and overwhelmed by the need around her. Sometimes she feels far away from her family up in the North East and wonders what God's plans will reveal next. Willingness to listen for God's plans, patience to work them out, courage to keep on going especially at times of feeling isolated and wondering why He works things out the way he does, continue to be essential ingredients in her life.

In every circuit where I have served some dear brother or sister has approached me within the first few weeks of our stay saying: 'We are so glad that you have come, but you need to realise that this is the hardest place in the Universe to be a Christian. This is the most godless part of Britain. This is the second most problematic housing estate in Europe. This is the one circuit in Methodism that finds it hard to attract and keep ministers. The congregations are divided, the preachers are boring, the coffers are empty and the buildings are derelict. There is a witches coven meeting on that hill and fifteen mosques have been opened in the last three years in this town...' When they are through, I thank them for their words of encouragement and reply that I have heard something similar to this of every place I have lived! I do not underrate the principalities and powers stacked against us. I wish to understand the context of our mission with realism rather than triumphalism, but I am convinced that there is no place and no one devoid of hope and opportunity. To believe such would be a denial of God's grace and the transforming power of the Gospel.

Time and again it is clear that God uses people who would regard themselves as rather unpromising material. He takes us not because of our vast gifts, our perfect theological grasp, or our ideal circumstances but because we are willing to do what he asks. That means taking risks, doing things which others will think (and occasionally say) are crazy - appearing foolish to be truly wise.

THINK THROUGH
1. *Write a life chart showing your faith journey from youth up to the present. Identify the difficult and wonderful parts of the route.*
   Alternatively, you could fold a piece of paper several times and cut small pieces out along the folds, then open it up to show that the cuts (painful parts) can form an attractive pattern of which you were not previously aware.
2. *Are there difficult times in your past you draw on to strengthen your faith today?*
3. *What is God calling us to in our present situation?*
   BIBLE BASE
   Luke 19 v. 1 - 10 - Zacchaeus, one of many unlikely followers.

9. PADDLING A BATTLESHIP

Getting evangelism and mission to the top of the local church's agenda in such a way that it becomes as natural as breathing has been described by one minister as like trying to steer a battleship with an oar strapped to the stern! Even after a decade of evangelism, we find that there has been more said than done, that most churches and leaders are locked into outdated models of being church and that training for preaching and ministry too often bypass our secular postmodern context. As most church leaders, following Robert Warren, tell us we need to move out of maintenance mode and into mission mode if we are to connect with contemporary society.

The institutional church in the West is undoubtedly crumbling and is being replaced with exciting new ways of being church which are contextualised and outward facing. As Barrie Cooke states in the recent video production for Methodist church planting, 'Stopping the Rot' - 'Growing churches find their focus outside themselves.'

Bishop Rowan Williams states that to speak of a Decade of Evangelism is 'a necessary idiocy - like declaring a decade of breathing.' Emil Brunner, for a former generation, wrote 'the church exists by mission as a fire exists by burning', yet for many congregations talk of evangelism and mission sounds like threatening innovation. Where the church has lost its founding purpose and come to operate more like a yachting club than a life boat station, it is exactly and necessarily this.

Recognising that congregations may need specialised help to become more missionary in intent and action, Methodism has appointed over several years a network of District Mission and Evangelism Enablers. They have different names and job descriptions in every District! Some are ordained, others are Lay. All have considerable experience in evangelism, some major on teaching and enabling, others on youth, some on preaching, others more facilitating. None would consider themselves as experts in the field of evangelism (and would be wary of anyone who felt they were!), though all have an enthusiasm for it. As they become established they are being used more widely in their Districts.

Who are these people and what do they do? Here are a few examples:

* Linda (Lou) Ashford is part time Mission Enabler in London South West District. Her emphasis has been on encouraging church members to share their faith one to one. Her teaching and preaching programmes major on this theme. Circuits have been disappointingly slow to take the opportunity of using Linda's gifts in the District but those who have done so have found the experience inspiring and encouraging.

* Ian White is the Sheffield District Mission Enabler. After ten years as East Anglia District Youth Evangelist, Ian came to Sheffield in January 1998. He has an office base at the Victoria Hall in the centre of the city and has set in motion several training and envisioning initiatives around the District. Ian has been instrumental in developing a Diploma in Children's Evangelism and Nurture validated by the University of Sheffield.

* Steve Wild follows ministry in the St Ives area with a District role combining working on religious broadcasts for West Country Television and being Mission Enabler in the whole county of Cornwall. He has a unique and inspiring evangelistic preaching ministry and an ability to communicate the Gospel effectively especially through the media.

Other Mission Enablers combine their role with circuit ministry or part time secular employment. The intention in every case is to better equip local congregations and their leaders for the mission task, recognising that the local church is the primary agent of mission. There is a continuing movement away from special campaigns and projects and towards commitment to on-going indigenous styles of mission which are relevant to and owned by local people, not imposed from afar.

It is good to note that other denominations are recognising the need for help in the building of missionary congregations. The United Reformed Church has appointed mission enablers, Baptists and Anglicans in differing ways are highlighting the work of the evangelist whilst at the same time affirming that all Christians have a role in evangelism as witnesses of Jesus Christ. These structural changes take a long time to have much effect and they depend on visionary local leadership which dreams the dream of the Kingdom and completes the sentence 'Wouldn't it be great if....' Local leadership must not be afraid to be unpopular with laggards, traditionalists and pessimists, combining prophecy and pastoral competence, communicating vision to initiate change. This change is painfully slow in many cases - but it is possible and it does happen. Even my friend with the oar on the stern of the battleship is recognising that!

THINK THROUGH
1. *How does your church live for the benefit of those who do not yet belong?*
2. *What changes in the church are necessary to reach and keep newcomers - especially young people?*
3. *Where is your deck chair on the ship?*
    - *up front, looking forward to new people and places*
    - *at the rear, viewing where you have been on a receding horizon*
    - *somewhere along the side, observing life as it passes by*
    - *or perhaps you are still trying to erect your deck chair!*

BIBLE BASE   *Ephesians 4 v. 1 - 16 - One Body with many parts.*

10. TEAM WORK

A significant feature of evangelistic strategy over recent years has been team work. This is in part a reaction against methods which seem to focus on a particular individual as the evangelist and partly a realisation that the best way to mentor and train people in evangelism is through team work. In such an environment it is possible for the strong to support the weak, the inexperienced to learn from the more experienced and for team members to test gifts in a safe and supportive environment.

These teams are therefore not made up of experts in evangelism, if such exist, but frequently of relatively new recruits to faith and mission. The vitality and vulnerability of these people is often their greatest asset, if harnessed by mature leadership. It involves great risks - new recruits can make some big mistakes. This is not the only way in which inexperienced people learn, and they need not do so at the expense of local receiving congregations, but the team environment certainly helps people to discover and use their gifts.

There is little new in the team concept: Jesus chose twelve and sent them out two by two, on another occasion his team expanded to seventy two. One would hardly say that these people were fully trained. They certainly hadn't seen the latest video on church planting, read this month's wisdom on how congregations grow, completed unit 19 on their preachers course or heard of Missiology! Ah, but they had been with Jesus, a great advantage we would expect!

They had heard him speak, seen him in action, been to places with him, shared in the ministry as they were able. Now they were on their own - in twos.... Preach the Good News, heal the sick, set free the captives, cast out the Devil, quite a challenging undertaking for raw recruits. They were to put the Gospel into action and then report back - 'unpack and reflect' in our hideous jargon - though they had no suitcases or mirrors and no need for extra sandals etc. Matthew 10 v5-20.

We see examples of the team approach in various guises since the first century and from monasticism to overseas missionary advance. Teams stand or fall on the quality of their support and leadership and on the degree to which they understand and connect with the host culture. Often teams are not around for long enough to appear much more than an invasion force which, like those before them, will come and go, and after which the host community can return to 'normality'. This is not to say that teams cannot be effective agents of mission - they can be, but their work is only valuable when it is part of the on going strategic missionary policy of local congregations. Teams have much to receive as well as to give. Bible and Theological College mission teams seek a partnership with local churches: visitors come to share with the existing local team/congregation in their on-going work.

The visitors certainly do not come to 'do' a mission for a church, though they will often be a means of priming the pump.

A great strength of team working is that it allows far more gifts to be realised than could possibly be found in one individual leader or missioner. A variety of ages and backgrounds is tremendously enriching. As in the church at Antioch in Acts 13, diversity may be their greatest strength. A culturally varied team can reach a mixed neighbourhood most effectively if varied views and styles can be held together without one part rubbishing the style or emphasis of another. The team can in fact help to focus the church more firmly on mission rather than on internal programmes and contentions.

Theological and Bible College, Share Jesus, Lay Witness and other missioning groups all operate on team principles. Whilst inexperience can be an advantage - naive questions are wonderfully challenging - damage can be done by poorly prepared or emotionally unstable individuals. Here again the role of team leader as co-ordinator of the team and mediator between team and church, is crucial.

A team that can model the diverse ministries of the Body of Christ can be a huge stimulus to local church members in using their gifts. Most team members are observably 'just normal people' and the challenge is that, if God can speak through them, he can probably speak through you and some others who may have gifts lying dormant. The use and discovery of these gifts will begin to challenge and change our way of being church into something less clerically dominated, more participatory and therefore in itself more team.

THINK THROUGH
1. *How can your congregation operate more as team?*
2. *What styles of leadership are necessary for good team work?*
3. *Might there be benefit in using a visiting mission team in the on-going mission of your church?*

BIBLE BASE
Acts 13 v. 1 - 3 - The Antioch church's diverse leadership team.
Colossians 4 v. 7 - 18 - Paul's team members and mission partners.

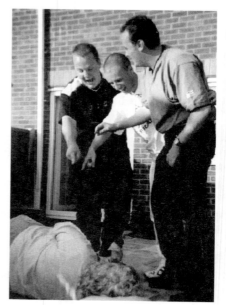

Street Theatre,
Manchester

11. BEYOND MISSION PRAISE

For those who find Mission Praise and Songs of Fellowship a little too radical for their taste in worship, or feel that by using such material they are on the cutting edge of contextualised evangelism, I have some news! Much of what passes for contemporary Christian music is almost as far removed from the culture of secular and younger people (and many of an older generation) as are the hymns of Wesley and Watts. If, having shared our faith with not yet Christians, we hope to expose them to worship which relates to the society in which we live and the questions about faith which arise in these contexts, we will need to think creatively about the way Christian worship and Gospel proclamation is packaged.

A recent survey of churches within Methodism, which had experienced sustained numerical growth during the last decade, highlighted the fact that one of the main reasons for this growth was a major commitment of time and creative energy to appropriate styles of worship. These styles varied and certainly could not be consigned to the so called 'happy clappy' category despised by some, but all indicated that we can do better than hymn sandwiches.

Youth evangelists and students at Cliff College have brought their technical and musical gifts to bear on late night worship events at the annual Derwent Week and Celebration Weekend held at the College. What had looked like a typical 1980's overgrown youth fellowship evening sing-along with a Gospel challenge has gradually been transformed into a contemporary youth worship experience. It not only attracts people from all parts of Britain who come to gain ideas and inspiration, but also brings young (and not so young) people to faith.

This has involved a huge investment of time on the part of artists, technical crew, musicians and others. Some have offered gifts in communication, in programming and unjamming computers, and in operating video projectors. Others have spent hours seeking out graphics and information from the internet, erecting and testing equipment, practising music for new songs, rehearsing drama etc. Many have prayed, several have given generously towards equipment costs, everyone has something to offer towards the goal of worshipping God in spirit and truth in a way which is authentic for those who find traditional forms of worship unsatisfying.

Most congregations will not have the resources in personnel or technology to attempt all of this - but it is not impossible for circuits and ecumenical groupings with a vision to reach the younger generation. Indeed there are several inspiring examples of this taking place. This is not just a style which relates to young people. Many older folk, from within and outside the church, find it refreshing and challenging. The presentation does not blast rock music at an audience. Many parts of the presentation are quiet and meditative. There is an emphasis on participation for those who wish to participate, but also space for those who prefer to observe. A clear Gospel presentation and often a challenge to make a physical response are integral aspects of the whole event. This response may be to a first step of commitment, or to a further step of faith, to vocation or social action. Salvation is a broad word - the Good News is for the whole creation and the call to response recognises this. At the close, counselling and prayer is available.

A Tour incorporating a scaled down version of this event has visited 25 venues around England. The concept has not been to put on a mega event to which Christians come, are impressed and then wait for the next time, but to put into the minds of those who attend the thought that 'we could do that'. This Tour has been the most effective mission style employed by Cliff College in recent years. Many have come to faith as they have heard the Gospel 'in their own language'. The latest development has been the production of a Compact Disc.

Whether or not this particular approach to worship is appropriate in your situation, it is vital that our desire for others to come to faith is reflected in the whole way that we operate as church. In no sense is this more true than in worship. Whilst I do not suggest that we ditch our rich heritage in favour of jumping onto passing bandwagons, a new arrival in a family causes disruption of routine and necessitates change. New Christians will require change in your church which is very threatening to those who love the institution and its procedures. Where there is an unwillingness to adapt to a new context, new life will migrate to where it can flourish. The only alternative to change is death - preservation of the past eventually turns into fossilisation. The Good News is that it doesn't have to be that way!

THINK THROUGH
1. *Who does our church seek to reach and who is our worship style culturally appropriate for?*
2. *What changes in life and worship may be necessary to enable the congregation to reach its neighbourhood? How might these be implemented?*
3. *How do we express ourselves in daily life? Is this carried over into our worship or are we being pushed into a certain mould?*

BIBLE BASE
Psalm 98 - Worship in the Spirit

12. CROSSING CULTURES - 'WOW!'

In August 1998, following three years of evangelistic training and waiting on God, Anne Houghton left a successful career as a radiographer in a West Midlands hospital to work amongst women and children in Ringili, Madi/West Nile Diocese, Arua, North West Uganda. Her testimony to God's call to the 'mission field' at her commissioning service at Four Oaks Methodist Church, Sutton Coldfield, where she has been an active member for many years, began: 'Wow!'. She feels to be one of the most unlikely people to be called to serve God in Africa, leaving behind the security of friends, a good job and a pleasant living environment.

In saying this she is like so many others of us who look back and marvel at the way God has guided us and, as we face the future with some trepidation, we face it also in the knowledge that 'those who God calls he equips'. His calling is often like an overcoat which we must grow into. At first we are 'swamped' by all that is new, but slowly we realise that we are in God's will: as events unfold, we see His hand. Guidance is easy with hindsight but scary in the present, even when we claim the promise that the God who has been with us through the valleys and the mountain tops of the past is the same God who will lead us into an unknown future.

You may be reading this knowing that it is impossible for you to ditch all your responsibilities and head for Africa - and you are probably right. Actually, it may be the harder option to work through your present circumstances and serve Christ in them, seeking his will from where you are now, rather than where you might like to be. Your call to run the toddlers group or the night shelter down the street is just as valid as a call to preach or travel to distant lands.

Evidently though, God is still raising up people to work alongside overseas partners in mission. Anne is linked to Africa Inland Mission, an interdenominational international missionary society established in 1895 and continuing with a vision of establishing the Gospel among hitherto unreached people groups in many parts of Africa. Anne's specific work is to equip pastors' wives for ministry and local churches to disciple children. Women's leadership, in the African context, has been almost ignored for mainly cultural reasons but new opportunities are now arising which recognise traditional patterns. The discipleship of children is crucial in a situation where over half the population are under 15 years of age and the need for education is paramount. In East Africa, as in many parts of the world, there has tended to be a stress in protestant churches on conversion rather than discipleship. Anne's role as an equipper of local churches is to help them to teach the Christian faith so that believers put down strong roots, understand the message of the Bible and apply faith to life.

In this teaching role, Anne is well aware that she learns as much as she teaches, giving but also receiving. The challenge of learning the local language, growing food crops near her hut and cooking with primitive equipment helps with this.

Authors such as Vincent Donovan have shown us, in his case from an East African context, that the cross cultural mission mindset needed for effective evangelisation in Africa is directly relevant to our mission strategy towards plural society in the 'developed world'. We will need to put the Gospel into a language which is understandable by people who have few building blocks of faith. We may need to ditch some cherished garments with which we have clothed the Gospel for a past generation. We may need to be much more vulnerable than we have been, to meet people where they are, rather in the Christian enclave - be that church, home group or mission station.

You may not need to swallow malaria pills to engage in this mission but, be sure, you will need to make some cross cultural leaps to get the Gospel out of the church and onto the pavement. Most people who have been to church all their lives have no conception of how huge a step it is from the pavement to the church. What kind of ramps will you put in place to make this more possible in your community? Of course, the steps are steep in both directions. If your theology of mission is merely about 'reaching them out there' and bringing them in to be where you are, then you need to be helped down the ramp yourself to meet not yet Christian people on their territory and on their terms. Jesus, 'friend of tax collectors and sinners' certainly did that - often to the dismay of the religious elite. The incarnation is about God alongside us - not shouting instructions and threats from a distance but becoming one of us. Love and identification were the hallmarks of his life and the Gospel just slipped out in every part of it as a result. The radical implications for our evangelism and for our lives are obvious.

THINK THROUGH
1. *What cross cultural issues do we face in Britain which make some methods of bridging the gap between Western and non-western cultures relevant for us in Britain here and now?*
2. *What might be the role of the white western missionary in the developing world today and how has this role changed in recent decades?*
3. *What if God called you to Africa?*

BIBLE BASE
Acts 17 v. 16 - 34 - Paul's approach to declaring the Gospel in a different culture.